50 Homemade Dessert Recipes for Home

By: Kelly Johnson

Table of Contents

- Classic Chocolate Chip Cookies
- Fudgy Brownies
- Vanilla Bean Cupcakes
- Lemon Bars
- Red Velvet Cake
- Blueberry Muffins
- Peanut Butter Blossoms
- Apple Crisp
- Carrot Cake with Cream Cheese Frosting
- Chocolate Lava Cake
- Raspberry Cheesecake Bars
- Snickerdoodle Cookies
- Banana Bread
- Key Lime Pie
- Oatmeal Raisin Cookies
- Strawberry Shortcake
- Pecan Pie
- Chocolate Covered Strawberries
- Coconut Macaroons
- Tiramisu
- Peanut Butter Fudge
- Peach Cobbler
- Molten Chocolate Cake
- Cinnamon Rolls
- Cheesecake Brownies
- Pumpkin Pie
- S'mores Bars
- Chocolate Truffles
- Cherry Pie
- Salted Caramel Brownies
- Apple Pie
- Rice Krispie Treats
- Chocolate Covered Pretzels
- Lemon Meringue Pie
- Black Forest Cake

- Peanut Butter Cookies
- Chocolate Pudding
- Strawberry Rhubarb Crisp
- Mint Chocolate Chip Ice Cream
- Blondies
- Raspberry Tart
- Chocolate Eclairs
- Apple Turnovers
- Caramel Popcorn
- Lemon Poppy Seed Cake
- Almond Biscotti
- Raspberry Chocolate Chip Cookies
- Chocolate Covered Bananas
- Coconut Cream Pie
- Coffee Cake

Classic Chocolate Chip Cookies

Ingredients:

- 1 cup (2 sticks) unsalted butter, at room temperature
- 3/4 cup granulated sugar
- 3/4 cup packed light brown sugar
- 2 large eggs
- 1 teaspoon vanilla extract
- 2 1/4 cups all-purpose flour
- 1 teaspoon baking soda
- 1/2 teaspoon salt
- 2 cups semisweet chocolate chips

Instructions:

1. Preheat your oven to 350°F (175°C). Line baking sheets with parchment paper or silicone baking mats.
2. In a large mixing bowl, cream together the butter, granulated sugar, and brown sugar until light and fluffy.
3. Beat in the eggs one at a time, then add the vanilla extract and mix until well combined.
4. In a separate bowl, whisk together the flour, baking soda, and salt.
5. Gradually add the dry ingredients to the wet ingredients, mixing until just combined.
6. Fold in the chocolate chips until evenly distributed throughout the dough.
7. Drop rounded tablespoons of dough onto the prepared baking sheets, spacing them about 2 inches apart.
8. Bake in the preheated oven for 9 to 11 minutes, or until the edges are lightly golden brown.
9. Remove from the oven and let the cookies cool on the baking sheets for a few minutes before transferring them to wire racks to cool completely.
10. Enjoy your delicious classic chocolate chip cookies with a glass of milk or your favorite beverage!

Fudgy Brownies

Ingredients:

- 1 cup (2 sticks) unsalted butter
- 2 cups granulated sugar
- 4 large eggs
- 1 teaspoon vanilla extract
- 3/4 cup unsweetened cocoa powder
- 1 cup all-purpose flour
- 1/2 teaspoon salt
- 1 cup semi-sweet chocolate chips (optional)

Instructions:

1. Preheat your oven to 350°F (175°C). Grease a 9x13-inch baking pan or line it with parchment paper.
2. In a microwave-safe bowl, melt the butter in the microwave in 30-second intervals until completely melted.
3. Stir in the granulated sugar until well combined.
4. Add the eggs, one at a time, mixing well after each addition. Stir in the vanilla extract.
5. Sift in the cocoa powder, flour, and salt. Mix until just combined. Be careful not to overmix.
6. If using, fold in the chocolate chips until evenly distributed in the batter.
7. Pour the batter into the prepared baking pan and spread it evenly with a spatula.
8. Bake in the preheated oven for 25-30 minutes, or until a toothpick inserted into the center comes out with a few moist crumbs.
9. Remove the brownies from the oven and let them cool completely in the pan on a wire rack.
10. Once cooled, cut into squares and serve. Enjoy your deliciously fudgy brownies!

Vanilla Bean Cupcakes

Ingredients:

- 1 3/4 cups all-purpose flour
- 1 1/2 teaspoons baking powder
- 1/2 teaspoon salt
- 1/2 cup (1 stick) unsalted butter, at room temperature
- 1 cup granulated sugar
- 2 large eggs, at room temperature
- 1 tablespoon vanilla bean paste or the seeds scraped from 1 vanilla bean pod
- 1/2 cup whole milk
- 1/4 cup sour cream or Greek yogurt

Instructions:

1. Preheat your oven to 350°F (175°C). Line a standard muffin tin with paper cupcake liners.
2. In a medium bowl, whisk together the flour, baking powder, and salt. Set aside.
3. In a large mixing bowl, cream together the butter and sugar until light and fluffy, using an electric mixer on medium speed.
4. Add the eggs one at a time, beating well after each addition. Mix in the vanilla bean paste or seeds until well combined.
5. Gradually add the dry ingredients to the wet ingredients, alternating with the milk, beginning and ending with the dry ingredients. Mix until just combined.
6. Stir in the sour cream or Greek yogurt until evenly incorporated into the batter.
7. Divide the batter evenly among the prepared cupcake liners, filling each about 2/3 full.
8. Bake in the preheated oven for 18 to 20 minutes, or until a toothpick inserted into the center of a cupcake comes out clean.
9. Remove the cupcakes from the oven and let them cool in the pan for a few minutes before transferring them to a wire rack to cool completely.
10. Once cooled, frost the cupcakes with your favorite frosting, if desired, and decorate as desired.
11. Serve and enjoy these deliciously moist and flavorful Vanilla Bean Cupcakes!

Lemon Bars

Ingredients:

For the crust:

- 1 cup all-purpose flour
- 1/2 cup unsalted butter, softened
- 1/4 cup powdered sugar

For the lemon filling:

- 1 cup granulated sugar
- 2 large eggs
- 1/3 cup freshly squeezed lemon juice (about 2-3 lemons)
- 1 tablespoon lemon zest
- 2 tablespoons all-purpose flour
- 1/2 teaspoon baking powder
- Powdered sugar, for dusting

Instructions:

1. Preheat your oven to 350°F (175°C). Grease or line an 8x8-inch baking dish with parchment paper, leaving an overhang on the sides for easy removal.
2. In a mixing bowl, combine the flour, softened butter, and powdered sugar for the crust. Mix until the mixture resembles coarse crumbs.
3. Press the crust mixture evenly into the bottom of the prepared baking dish. Bake in the preheated oven for 15-18 minutes, or until lightly golden brown.
4. While the crust is baking, prepare the lemon filling. In another mixing bowl, whisk together the granulated sugar and eggs until well combined.
5. Add the freshly squeezed lemon juice and lemon zest to the sugar and egg mixture, and whisk until smooth.
6. In a separate bowl, sift together the flour and baking powder. Gradually add the dry ingredients to the wet ingredients, whisking until smooth and well combined.
7. Once the crust is baked, remove it from the oven and pour the lemon filling evenly over the hot crust.

8. Return the baking dish to the oven and bake for an additional 20-25 minutes, or until the lemon filling is set and the edges are lightly golden brown.
9. Remove the lemon bars from the oven and let them cool completely in the baking dish on a wire rack.
10. Once cooled, dust the top of the lemon bars with powdered sugar. Use the parchment paper overhang to lift the bars out of the dish and onto a cutting board.
11. Cut into squares or rectangles and serve. Enjoy these tangy and sweet Lemon Bars as a delightful treat!

Red Velvet Cake

Ingredients:

For the cake:

- 2 1/2 cups all-purpose flour
- 1 1/2 cups granulated sugar
- 1 teaspoon baking soda
- 1 teaspoon salt
- 1 teaspoon cocoa powder
- 1 1/2 cups vegetable oil
- 1 cup buttermilk, at room temperature
- 2 large eggs, at room temperature
- 2 tablespoons red food coloring
- 1 teaspoon vanilla extract
- 1 teaspoon white vinegar

For the cream cheese frosting:

- 16 ounces cream cheese, softened
- 1/2 cup (1 stick) unsalted butter, softened
- 4 cups powdered sugar, sifted
- 1 teaspoon vanilla extract

Instructions:

1. Preheat your oven to 350°F (175°C). Grease and flour two 9-inch round cake pans, or line them with parchment paper.
2. In a medium bowl, sift together the flour, sugar, baking soda, salt, and cocoa powder.
3. In a large mixing bowl, whisk together the vegetable oil, buttermilk, eggs, red food coloring, vanilla extract, and white vinegar until well combined.
4. Gradually add the dry ingredients to the wet ingredients, mixing until smooth and well combined.
5. Divide the batter evenly between the prepared cake pans, spreading it out evenly with a spatula.

6. Bake in the preheated oven for 25-30 minutes, or until a toothpick inserted into the center of the cakes comes out clean.
7. Remove the cakes from the oven and let them cool in the pans for 10 minutes before transferring them to wire racks to cool completely.
8. While the cakes are cooling, prepare the cream cheese frosting. In a large mixing bowl, beat together the softened cream cheese and butter until smooth and creamy.
9. Gradually add the powdered sugar, one cup at a time, beating well after each addition. Stir in the vanilla extract until smooth and creamy.
10. Once the cakes are completely cooled, place one cake layer on a serving plate or cake stand. Spread a layer of cream cheese frosting on top.
11. Place the second cake layer on top of the frosting and frost the top and sides of the cake with the remaining cream cheese frosting.
12. If desired, decorate the cake with red velvet cake crumbs or other decorations.
13. Slice and serve the delicious and moist Red Velvet Cake! Enjoy!

Blueberry Muffins

Ingredients:

- 2 cups all-purpose flour
- 1/2 cup granulated sugar
- 2 teaspoons baking powder
- 1/2 teaspoon baking soda
- 1/4 teaspoon salt
- 1/2 cup unsalted butter, melted and cooled
- 2 large eggs, at room temperature
- 1 cup buttermilk, at room temperature
- 1 teaspoon vanilla extract
- 1 1/2 cups fresh or frozen blueberries
- Turbinado sugar (optional, for topping)

Instructions:

1. Preheat your oven to 375°F (190°C). Line a muffin tin with paper liners or grease each cup lightly with butter or cooking spray.
2. In a large mixing bowl, whisk together the flour, sugar, baking powder, baking soda, and salt until well combined.
3. In another bowl, whisk together the melted butter, eggs, buttermilk, and vanilla extract until smooth and well combined.
4. Pour the wet ingredients into the dry ingredients and gently fold them together using a rubber spatula until just combined. Be careful not to overmix; it's okay if there are a few lumps in the batter.
5. Gently fold in the blueberries until evenly distributed throughout the batter.
6. Divide the batter evenly among the prepared muffin cups, filling each about 2/3 to 3/4 full.
7. If desired, sprinkle a little turbinado sugar over the tops of the muffins for a crunchy topping.
8. Bake in the preheated oven for 18-22 minutes, or until the muffins are golden brown and a toothpick inserted into the center comes out clean.
9. Remove the muffins from the oven and let them cool in the muffin tin for a few minutes before transferring them to a wire rack to cool completely.
10. Serve the delicious blueberry muffins warm or at room temperature. Enjoy!

Peanut Butter Blossoms

Ingredients:

- 1/2 cup (1 stick) unsalted butter, softened
- 3/4 cup creamy peanut butter
- 1/3 cup granulated sugar
- 1/3 cup packed light brown sugar
- 1 large egg
- 1 teaspoon vanilla extract
- 1 1/2 cups all-purpose flour
- 1 teaspoon baking soda
- 1/2 teaspoon salt
- 1/4 cup granulated sugar (for rolling)
- 36 Hershey's Kisses, unwrapped

Instructions:

1. Preheat your oven to 375°F (190°C). Line baking sheets with parchment paper or silicone baking mats.
2. In a large mixing bowl, cream together the softened butter, creamy peanut butter, granulated sugar, and brown sugar until light and fluffy.
3. Add the egg and vanilla extract to the peanut butter mixture and beat until well combined.
4. In a separate bowl, whisk together the flour, baking soda, and salt.
5. Gradually add the dry ingredients to the wet ingredients, mixing until just combined.
6. Shape the dough into 1-inch balls and roll them in the granulated sugar to coat evenly.
7. Place the sugar-coated dough balls on the prepared baking sheets, spacing them about 2 inches apart.
8. Bake in the preheated oven for 8-10 minutes, or until the edges are set and the cookies are slightly golden brown.
9. Remove the baking sheets from the oven and immediately press a Hershey's Kiss into the center of each cookie, pressing down slightly so that the cookie cracks around the edges.

10. Let the cookies cool on the baking sheets for a few minutes before transferring them to wire racks to cool completely.
11. Once cooled, store the Peanut Butter Blossoms in an airtight container at room temperature for up to one week. Enjoy!

Apple Crisp

Ingredients:

For the apple filling:

- 6 cups peeled, cored, and sliced apples (such as Granny Smith or Honeycrisp)
- 1/4 cup granulated sugar
- 1 tablespoon lemon juice
- 1 teaspoon ground cinnamon
- 1/4 teaspoon ground nutmeg
- 1/4 teaspoon salt

For the crisp topping:

- 1 cup old-fashioned rolled oats
- 1/2 cup all-purpose flour
- 1/2 cup packed light brown sugar
- 1/2 teaspoon ground cinnamon
- 1/4 teaspoon salt
- 1/2 cup (1 stick) unsalted butter, cold and cubed

Instructions:

1. Preheat your oven to 350°F (175°C). Grease a 9x13-inch baking dish or a similar-sized baking dish.
2. In a large mixing bowl, toss together the sliced apples, granulated sugar, lemon juice, ground cinnamon, ground nutmeg, and salt until well combined. Transfer the apple mixture to the prepared baking dish and spread it out evenly.
3. In a separate mixing bowl, combine the old-fashioned rolled oats, all-purpose flour, packed light brown sugar, ground cinnamon, and salt for the crisp topping. Mix until well combined.
4. Add the cold, cubed butter to the crisp topping mixture. Using your fingers or a pastry cutter, work the butter into the dry ingredients until the mixture resembles coarse crumbs and the butter is evenly distributed.
5. Sprinkle the crisp topping evenly over the apple mixture in the baking dish, covering it completely.

6. Bake in the preheated oven for 40-45 minutes, or until the topping is golden brown and the apples are tender and bubbling.
7. Remove the apple crisp from the oven and let it cool for a few minutes before serving.
8. Serve the apple crisp warm with a scoop of vanilla ice cream or a dollop of whipped cream, if desired. Enjoy the comforting and delicious flavors of this classic dessert!

Carrot Cake with Cream Cheese Frosting

Ingredients:

For the carrot cake:

- 2 cups all-purpose flour
- 2 teaspoons baking powder
- 1 teaspoon baking soda
- 1/2 teaspoon salt
- 2 teaspoons ground cinnamon
- 1/2 teaspoon ground nutmeg
- 1/2 teaspoon ground ginger
- 1 cup granulated sugar
- 1 cup packed light brown sugar
- 1 cup vegetable oil
- 4 large eggs
- 2 teaspoons vanilla extract
- 3 cups grated carrots (about 4-5 medium carrots)
- 1 cup chopped walnuts or pecans (optional)
- 1/2 cup crushed pineapple, drained (optional)

For the cream cheese frosting:

- 1/2 cup (1 stick) unsalted butter, softened
- 8 ounces cream cheese, softened
- 4 cups powdered sugar, sifted
- 2 teaspoons vanilla extract

Instructions:

1. Preheat your oven to 350°F (175°C). Grease and flour two 9-inch round cake pans or line them with parchment paper.
2. In a large mixing bowl, sift together the flour, baking powder, baking soda, salt, cinnamon, nutmeg, and ginger.
3. In another mixing bowl, whisk together the granulated sugar, brown sugar, vegetable oil, eggs, and vanilla extract until well combined.

4. Gradually add the dry ingredients to the wet ingredients, mixing until just combined.
5. Fold in the grated carrots, chopped nuts (if using), and crushed pineapple (if using) until evenly distributed in the batter.
6. Divide the batter evenly between the prepared cake pans, spreading it out evenly with a spatula.
7. Bake in the preheated oven for 25-30 minutes, or until a toothpick inserted into the center of the cakes comes out clean.
8. Remove the cakes from the oven and let them cool in the pans for 10 minutes before transferring them to wire racks to cool completely.
9. While the cakes are cooling, prepare the cream cheese frosting. In a large mixing bowl, beat together the softened butter and cream cheese until smooth and creamy.
10. Gradually add the powdered sugar, one cup at a time, beating well after each addition. Stir in the vanilla extract until smooth and creamy.
11. Once the cakes are completely cooled, place one cake layer on a serving plate or cake stand. Spread a layer of cream cheese frosting on top.
12. Place the second cake layer on top of the frosting and frost the top and sides of the cake with the remaining cream cheese frosting.
13. If desired, decorate the cake with additional grated carrots or chopped nuts.
14. Slice and serve the delicious and moist Carrot Cake with Cream Cheese Frosting! Enjoy!

Chocolate Lava Cake

Ingredients:

- 1/2 cup (1 stick) unsalted butter
- 4 ounces semi-sweet chocolate, chopped
- 2 large eggs
- 2 large egg yolks
- 1/4 cup granulated sugar
- 2 teaspoons vanilla extract
- 1/4 cup all-purpose flour
- Pinch of salt
- Cocoa powder or powdered sugar, for dusting (optional)
- Fresh berries or vanilla ice cream, for serving (optional)

Instructions:

1. Preheat your oven to 425°F (220°C). Grease four 6-ounce ramekins or custard cups with butter and dust them lightly with cocoa powder or powdered sugar. Place them on a baking sheet.
2. In a microwave-safe bowl, melt the butter and chopped semi-sweet chocolate together in the microwave in 30-second intervals, stirring after each interval, until smooth and completely melted. Set aside to cool slightly.
3. In a mixing bowl, whisk together the eggs, egg yolks, granulated sugar, and vanilla extract until well combined and slightly thickened.
4. Gradually pour the melted chocolate mixture into the egg mixture, whisking constantly until smooth and well combined.
5. Sift the all-purpose flour and salt over the chocolate mixture and gently fold them in until just combined. Be careful not to overmix.
6. Divide the batter evenly among the prepared ramekins, filling each about 3/4 full.
7. Bake in the preheated oven for 12-14 minutes, or until the edges are set but the centers are still soft and slightly jiggly.
8. Remove the lava cakes from the oven and let them cool in the ramekins for 1-2 minutes.
9. To serve, run a knife around the edges of each ramekin to loosen the cakes. Carefully invert each lava cake onto a serving plate.

10. Dust with cocoa powder or powdered sugar, if desired. Serve immediately with fresh berries or a scoop of vanilla ice cream on the side, if desired.
11. Enjoy these decadent Chocolate Lava Cakes while they are warm and gooey in the center!

Raspberry Cheesecake Bars

Ingredients:

For the crust:

- 1 1/2 cups graham cracker crumbs
- 1/4 cup granulated sugar
- 1/2 cup unsalted butter, melted

For the cheesecake filling:

- 16 ounces cream cheese, softened
- 1/2 cup granulated sugar
- 2 large eggs
- 1 teaspoon vanilla extract
- 1/4 cup sour cream

For the raspberry swirl:

- 1 cup fresh or frozen raspberries
- 2 tablespoons granulated sugar
- 1 tablespoon water
- 1 teaspoon cornstarch

Instructions:

1. Preheat your oven to 350°F (175°C). Grease or line an 8x8-inch baking dish with parchment paper, leaving an overhang on the sides for easy removal.
2. In a mixing bowl, combine the graham cracker crumbs, granulated sugar, and melted butter for the crust. Mix until well combined.
3. Press the crust mixture evenly into the bottom of the prepared baking dish. Bake in the preheated oven for 8-10 minutes, or until lightly golden brown. Remove from the oven and set aside to cool slightly.
4. In another mixing bowl, beat the softened cream cheese and granulated sugar together until smooth and creamy.

5. Add the eggs one at a time, beating well after each addition. Stir in the vanilla extract and sour cream until smooth and well combined.
6. Pour the cheesecake filling over the partially baked crust in the baking dish, spreading it out evenly with a spatula.
7. In a small saucepan, combine the raspberries, granulated sugar, water, and cornstarch. Cook over medium heat, stirring constantly, until the mixture thickens and the raspberries break down, about 5 minutes. Remove from heat and let it cool slightly.
8. Spoon dollops of the raspberry mixture over the cheesecake filling in the baking dish. Use a knife or skewer to swirl the raspberry mixture into the cheesecake filling.
9. Bake in the preheated oven for 30-35 minutes, or until the edges are set and the center is slightly jiggly.
10. Remove the raspberry cheesecake bars from the oven and let them cool completely in the baking dish on a wire rack.
11. Once cooled, refrigerate the bars for at least 2 hours, or until chilled and set.
12. Once chilled, use the parchment paper overhang to lift the bars out of the baking dish. Cut into squares and serve.
13. Enjoy these delicious Raspberry Cheesecake Bars as a delightful dessert or snack!

Snickerdoodle Cookies

Ingredients:

For the cookie dough:

- 2 3/4 cups all-purpose flour
- 2 teaspoons cream of tartar
- 1 teaspoon baking soda
- 1/4 teaspoon salt
- 1 cup (2 sticks) unsalted butter, softened
- 1 1/2 cups granulated sugar
- 2 large eggs
- 1 teaspoon vanilla extract

For the cinnamon-sugar coating:

- 1/4 cup granulated sugar
- 2 tablespoons ground cinnamon

Instructions:

1. Preheat your oven to 375°F (190°C). Line baking sheets with parchment paper or silicone baking mats.
2. In a medium bowl, whisk together the flour, cream of tartar, baking soda, and salt until well combined. Set aside.
3. In a large mixing bowl, cream together the softened butter and granulated sugar until light and fluffy, using an electric mixer on medium speed.
4. Add the eggs one at a time, beating well after each addition. Stir in the vanilla extract until well combined.
5. Gradually add the dry ingredients to the wet ingredients, mixing until just combined.
6. In a small bowl, mix together the granulated sugar and ground cinnamon for the coating.
7. Shape the cookie dough into 1-inch balls and roll them in the cinnamon-sugar mixture until evenly coated.

8. Place the coated dough balls on the prepared baking sheets, spacing them about 2 inches apart.
9. Flatten each dough ball slightly with the bottom of a glass or the palm of your hand.
10. Bake in the preheated oven for 8-10 minutes, or until the edges are set and the tops are slightly cracked.
11. Remove the cookies from the oven and let them cool on the baking sheets for a few minutes before transferring them to wire racks to cool completely.
12. Once cooled, store the Snickerdoodle Cookies in an airtight container at room temperature for up to one week.
13. Enjoy these classic and delicious Snickerdoodle Cookies with a glass of milk or your favorite beverage!

Banana Bread

Ingredients:

- 2 cups all-purpose flour
- 1 teaspoon baking soda
- 1/4 teaspoon salt
- 1/2 cup (1 stick) unsalted butter, softened
- 3/4 cup granulated sugar
- 2 large eggs
- 1 teaspoon vanilla extract
- 3 ripe bananas, mashed (about 1 1/2 cups)
- 1/4 cup sour cream or plain Greek yogurt

Optional add-ins:

- 1/2 cup chopped nuts (such as walnuts or pecans)
- 1/2 cup chocolate chips
- 1/2 cup dried fruit (such as raisins or cranberries)

Instructions:

1. Preheat your oven to 350°F (175°C). Grease a 9x5-inch loaf pan or line it with parchment paper.
2. In a medium bowl, whisk together the flour, baking soda, and salt. Set aside.
3. In a large mixing bowl, cream together the softened butter and granulated sugar until light and fluffy, using an electric mixer on medium speed.
4. Add the eggs one at a time, beating well after each addition. Stir in the vanilla extract until well combined.
5. Add the mashed bananas and sour cream or yogurt to the butter mixture, and mix until well combined.
6. Gradually add the dry ingredients to the wet ingredients, mixing until just combined. Be careful not to overmix.
7. If using, fold in the chopped nuts, chocolate chips, or dried fruit until evenly distributed in the batter.
8. Pour the batter into the prepared loaf pan, spreading it out evenly with a spatula.

9. Bake in the preheated oven for 50-60 minutes, or until a toothpick inserted into the center comes out clean.
10. Remove the banana bread from the oven and let it cool in the pan for 10-15 minutes before transferring it to a wire rack to cool completely.
11. Once cooled, slice and serve the delicious banana bread. Enjoy it warm or at room temperature, with a pat of butter if desired!
12. Store any leftovers in an airtight container at room temperature for up to three days, or freeze for longer storage.

Key Lime Pie

Ingredients:

For the crust:

- 1 1/2 cups graham cracker crumbs
- 1/4 cup granulated sugar
- 1/2 cup (1 stick) unsalted butter, melted

For the filling:

- 4 large egg yolks
- 14 ounces sweetened condensed milk
- 1/2 cup freshly squeezed key lime juice (about 20-25 key limes)
- 1 tablespoon grated key lime zest

For the whipped cream topping (optional):

- 1 cup heavy cream
- 2 tablespoons powdered sugar
- 1 teaspoon vanilla extract

Instructions:

1. Preheat your oven to 350°F (175°C). Grease a 9-inch pie dish.
2. In a mixing bowl, combine the graham cracker crumbs, granulated sugar, and melted butter for the crust. Mix until well combined.
3. Press the crust mixture evenly into the bottom and up the sides of the prepared pie dish.
4. Bake the crust in the preheated oven for 8-10 minutes, or until lightly golden brown. Remove from the oven and let it cool while you prepare the filling.
5. In a separate mixing bowl, whisk together the egg yolks and sweetened condensed milk until smooth.
6. Gradually whisk in the key lime juice and grated key lime zest until well combined.
7. Pour the filling mixture into the cooled graham cracker crust.
8. Bake the pie in the preheated oven for 15-17 minutes, or until the filling is set but still slightly jiggly in the center.

9. Remove the pie from the oven and let it cool completely on a wire rack. Once cooled, refrigerate the pie for at least 2 hours, or until chilled and set.
10. While the pie is chilling, prepare the whipped cream topping (if using). In a mixing bowl, beat the heavy cream, powdered sugar, and vanilla extract together until stiff peaks form.
11. Once the pie is chilled and set, spread or pipe the whipped cream over the top of the pie.
12. Slice and serve the delicious Key Lime Pie chilled, with extra whipped cream on top if desired. Enjoy the tangy and refreshing flavors!

Oatmeal Raisin Cookies

Ingredients:

- 1 cup (2 sticks) unsalted butter, softened
- 1 cup packed light brown sugar
- 1/2 cup granulated sugar
- 2 large eggs
- 1 teaspoon vanilla extract
- 1 1/2 cups all-purpose flour
- 1 teaspoon baking soda
- 1 teaspoon ground cinnamon
- 1/2 teaspoon salt
- 3 cups old-fashioned rolled oats
- 1 cup raisins

Instructions:

1. Preheat your oven to 350°F (175°C). Line baking sheets with parchment paper or silicone baking mats.
2. In a large mixing bowl, cream together the softened butter, packed light brown sugar, and granulated sugar until light and fluffy, using an electric mixer on medium speed.
3. Add the eggs one at a time, beating well after each addition. Stir in the vanilla extract until well combined.
4. In a separate bowl, whisk together the all-purpose flour, baking soda, ground cinnamon, and salt.
5. Gradually add the dry ingredients to the wet ingredients, mixing until just combined.
6. Stir in the old-fashioned rolled oats and raisins until evenly distributed in the cookie dough.
7. Drop tablespoonfuls of dough onto the prepared baking sheets, spacing them about 2 inches apart. You can also use a cookie scoop for evenly sized cookies.
8. Bake in the preheated oven for 10-12 minutes, or until the edges are lightly golden brown and the centers are set.
9. Remove the cookies from the oven and let them cool on the baking sheets for a few minutes before transferring them to wire racks to cool completely.

10. Once cooled, store the Oatmeal Raisin Cookies in an airtight container at room temperature for up to one week.
11. Enjoy these classic and delicious cookies with a glass of milk or your favorite beverage!

Strawberry Shortcake

Ingredients:

For the shortcakes:

- 2 cups all-purpose flour
- 1/4 cup granulated sugar
- 1 tablespoon baking powder
- 1/2 teaspoon salt
- 1/2 cup (1 stick) unsalted butter, cold and cut into small pieces
- 2/3 cup milk
- 1 teaspoon vanilla extract

For the strawberries:

- 1 pound fresh strawberries, hulled and sliced
- 2-3 tablespoons granulated sugar (adjust to taste)
- 1 teaspoon lemon juice

For the whipped cream:

- 1 cup heavy cream, chilled
- 2 tablespoons powdered sugar
- 1 teaspoon vanilla extract

Instructions:

1. Preheat your oven to 425°F (220°C). Line a baking sheet with parchment paper or silicone baking mats.
2. In a large mixing bowl, whisk together the flour, granulated sugar, baking powder, and salt.
3. Cut in the cold butter using a pastry cutter or your fingers until the mixture resembles coarse crumbs.
4. In a small bowl, combine the milk and vanilla extract. Gradually add the milk mixture to the dry ingredients, stirring with a fork until a dough forms.
5. Turn the dough out onto a lightly floured surface and gently knead it a few times until it comes together. Be careful not to overwork the dough.

6. Pat the dough into a circle about 1-inch thick. Use a biscuit cutter or a glass to cut out rounds of dough.
7. Place the dough rounds onto the prepared baking sheet, spacing them about 2 inches apart.
8. Bake in the preheated oven for 12-15 minutes, or until the shortcakes are golden brown and cooked through.
9. While the shortcakes are baking, prepare the strawberries. In a mixing bowl, combine the sliced strawberries, granulated sugar, and lemon juice. Toss until the strawberries are well coated. Let them macerate at room temperature while the shortcakes cool.
10. To make the whipped cream, beat the chilled heavy cream, powdered sugar, and vanilla extract together in a mixing bowl until stiff peaks form.
11. Once the shortcakes have cooled slightly, split them in half horizontally using a serrated knife.
12. To assemble, place a spoonful of strawberries on the bottom half of each shortcake. Top with a dollop of whipped cream and then place the top half of the shortcake on top.
13. Serve immediately and enjoy the delicious homemade Strawberry Shortcake!

Pecan Pie

Ingredients:

For the crust:

- 1 1/4 cups all-purpose flour
- 1/2 teaspoon salt
- 1/2 teaspoon granulated sugar
- 1/2 cup (1 stick) unsalted butter, cold and cut into small pieces
- 3 to 4 tablespoons ice water

For the filling:

- 1 cup granulated sugar
- 1 cup light corn syrup
- 1/2 cup unsalted butter, melted and cooled slightly
- 1 teaspoon vanilla extract
- 1/4 teaspoon salt
- 3 large eggs
- 1 1/2 cups pecan halves

Instructions:

1. Preheat your oven to 350°F (175°C). Place a baking sheet in the oven to preheat as well.
2. To make the crust, in a large mixing bowl, whisk together the flour, salt, and granulated sugar. Add the cold, cubed butter and use a pastry cutter or your fingers to cut the butter into the flour mixture until it resembles coarse crumbs.
3. Gradually add the ice water, 1 tablespoon at a time, mixing with a fork until the dough comes together. Be careful not to overwork the dough. Shape the dough into a disk, wrap it in plastic wrap, and refrigerate for at least 30 minutes.
4. On a lightly floured surface, roll out the chilled dough into a circle about 12 inches in diameter. Carefully transfer the dough to a 9-inch pie dish, pressing it gently into the bottom and sides of the dish. Trim any excess dough and crimp the edges as desired. Place the pie dish in the refrigerator while you prepare the filling.

5. In a large mixing bowl, whisk together the granulated sugar, light corn syrup, melted butter, vanilla extract, and salt until well combined.
6. Add the eggs one at a time, mixing well after each addition.
7. Stir in the pecan halves until evenly coated in the filling mixture.
8. Pour the pecan filling into the prepared pie crust.
9. Place the pie dish on the preheated baking sheet in the oven. Bake for 50 to 60 minutes, or until the filling is set and the crust is golden brown. If the edges of the crust start to brown too quickly, you can cover them with foil halfway through baking.
10. Remove the pecan pie from the oven and let it cool completely on a wire rack before slicing and serving.
11. Serve the delicious Pecan Pie at room temperature or slightly warmed, optionally with a dollop of whipped cream or a scoop of vanilla ice cream on top. Enjoy!

Chocolate Covered Strawberries

Ingredients:

- 1 pound fresh strawberries, rinsed and dried thoroughly
- 8 ounces semi-sweet chocolate, chopped (or chocolate chips)
- Optional toppings: chopped nuts, sprinkles, shredded coconut, or edible glitter

Instructions:

1. Line a baking sheet with parchment paper or wax paper.
2. Place the chopped chocolate in a heatproof bowl. Microwave it in 30-second intervals, stirring after each interval, until the chocolate is melted and smooth. Alternatively, you can melt the chocolate using a double boiler.
3. Hold a strawberry by the stem and dip it into the melted chocolate, swirling to coat it evenly. Allow any excess chocolate to drip back into the bowl.
4. If desired, roll the chocolate-covered strawberry in optional toppings, such as chopped nuts, sprinkles, shredded coconut, or edible glitter, while the chocolate is still wet.
5. Place the dipped strawberries on the prepared baking sheet, leaving a small space between each one.
6. Once all the strawberries are dipped and decorated, refrigerate them for about 30 minutes, or until the chocolate is set.
7. After the chocolate has set, transfer the chocolate-covered strawberries to an airtight container and store them in the refrigerator until ready to serve.
8. Enjoy these delicious and elegant Chocolate Covered Strawberries as a delightful treat or as a beautiful addition to any dessert platter or special occasion!

Coconut Macaroons

Ingredients:

- 3 cups sweetened shredded coconut
- 2/3 cup granulated sugar
- 1/4 teaspoon salt
- 4 large egg whites
- 1 teaspoon vanilla extract
- Optional: 4 ounces semi-sweet or bittersweet chocolate, melted (for dipping)

Instructions:

1. Preheat your oven to 325°F (160°C). Line a baking sheet with parchment paper or a silicone baking mat.
2. In a large mixing bowl, combine the sweetened shredded coconut, granulated sugar, and salt. Mix well.
3. In a separate bowl, whisk the egg whites and vanilla extract together until frothy.
4. Pour the egg white mixture over the coconut mixture and stir until well combined and the coconut is evenly moistened.
5. Using a spoon or cookie scoop, drop tablespoonfuls of the coconut mixture onto the prepared baking sheet, spacing them about 1 inch apart.
6. Using slightly wet hands, shape and compact each mound of coconut mixture into a rounded shape, pressing firmly to ensure they hold together during baking.
7. Bake in the preheated oven for 20-25 minutes, or until the macaroons are lightly golden brown on the edges and bottom.
8. Remove the macaroons from the oven and let them cool on the baking sheet for a few minutes before transferring them to a wire rack to cool completely.
9. If desired, drizzle or dip the cooled macaroons in melted chocolate. Allow the chocolate to set before serving.
10. Store the coconut macaroons in an airtight container at room temperature for up to one week. Enjoy these sweet and chewy treats!

Tiramisu

Ingredients:

- 6 large egg yolks
- 3/4 cup granulated sugar
- 1 cup mascarpone cheese, softened
- 1 1/2 cups heavy cream
- 1 teaspoon vanilla extract
- 1 1/2 cups strong brewed coffee, cooled to room temperature
- 2 tablespoons coffee liqueur (such as Kahlua or Tia Maria)
- 24-30 ladyfinger cookies (savoiardi)
- Unsweetened cocoa powder, for dusting

Instructions:

1. In a heatproof bowl, whisk together the egg yolks and granulated sugar until pale and thickened.
2. Place the bowl over a pot of simmering water (double boiler) and continue to whisk constantly until the mixture reaches 160°F (71°C) and thickens enough to coat the back of a spoon.
3. Remove the bowl from the heat and let it cool slightly.
4. In a separate mixing bowl, beat the mascarpone cheese until smooth and creamy.
5. In another mixing bowl, whip the heavy cream and vanilla extract together until stiff peaks form.
6. Gently fold the whipped cream into the mascarpone cheese until well combined.
7. Gradually fold the egg yolk mixture into the mascarpone and whipped cream mixture until smooth and creamy. Be gentle to avoid deflating the mixture.
8. In a shallow dish, combine the cooled brewed coffee and coffee liqueur.
9. Quickly dip each ladyfinger cookie into the coffee mixture, making sure not to soak them too long or they will become too soggy.
10. Arrange a layer of dipped ladyfinger cookies in the bottom of a 9x13-inch baking dish or a similar-sized dish, breaking them if necessary to fit.
11. Spread half of the mascarpone mixture evenly over the layer of ladyfingers.
12. Repeat with another layer of dipped ladyfingers and the remaining mascarpone mixture.

13. Cover the dish with plastic wrap and refrigerate for at least 4 hours, or preferably overnight, to allow the flavors to meld and the tiramisu to set.
14. Before serving, dust the top of the tiramisu with unsweetened cocoa powder using a fine-mesh sieve.
15. Slice and serve the delicious homemade Tiramisu chilled, and enjoy the rich and creamy layers of this classic Italian dessert!

Peanut Butter Fudge

Ingredients:

- 1 cup creamy peanut butter
- 1 cup unsalted butter
- 1 teaspoon vanilla extract
- 1 pound (about 4 cups) powdered sugar
- Optional: chopped peanuts for garnish

Instructions:

1. Line an 8x8-inch baking dish with parchment paper or aluminum foil, leaving some overhang on the sides for easy removal later. Lightly grease the lined dish with butter or non-stick cooking spray.
2. In a microwave-safe bowl, combine the peanut butter and unsalted butter. Microwave in 30-second intervals, stirring after each interval, until the mixture is melted and smooth.
3. Stir in the vanilla extract until well combined.
4. Gradually add the powdered sugar to the peanut butter mixture, stirring until smooth and well combined. The mixture will be thick.
5. Pour the fudge mixture into the prepared baking dish, spreading it out evenly with a spatula.
6. If desired, sprinkle chopped peanuts over the top of the fudge for garnish.
7. Refrigerate the fudge for at least 2 hours, or until firm and set.
8. Once the fudge is set, use the overhanging parchment paper or aluminum foil to lift it out of the baking dish. Place it on a cutting board and cut into squares or rectangles.
9. Serve and enjoy the creamy and delicious Peanut Butter Fudge! Store any leftovers in an airtight container in the refrigerator for up to one week.

Peach Cobbler

Ingredients:

For the peach filling:

- 6 cups sliced fresh or canned peaches (about 6-8 peaches)
- 1/2 cup granulated sugar (adjust to taste depending on sweetness of peaches)
- 1 tablespoon lemon juice
- 1 teaspoon vanilla extract
- 2 tablespoons cornstarch

For the cobbler topping:

- 1 cup all-purpose flour
- 1/2 cup granulated sugar
- 1 teaspoon baking powder
- 1/4 teaspoon salt
- 1/2 cup (1 stick) unsalted butter, melted
- 1/4 cup milk
- Optional: vanilla ice cream or whipped cream for serving

Instructions:

1. Preheat your oven to 375°F (190°C). Grease a 9x13-inch baking dish or similar-sized dish.
2. In a large mixing bowl, combine the sliced peaches, granulated sugar, lemon juice, vanilla extract, and cornstarch. Toss until the peaches are well coated.
3. Pour the peach mixture into the prepared baking dish, spreading it out evenly.
4. In another mixing bowl, whisk together the flour, granulated sugar, baking powder, and salt for the cobbler topping.
5. Add the melted butter and milk to the dry ingredients, and stir until just combined. The batter will be thick.
6. Drop spoonfuls of the cobbler batter over the top of the peach mixture in the baking dish, spreading it out evenly with a spatula.
7. Bake in the preheated oven for 35-40 minutes, or until the cobbler topping is golden brown and the peach filling is bubbly around the edges.

8. Remove the peach cobbler from the oven and let it cool for a few minutes before serving.
9. Serve the warm Peach Cobbler with a scoop of vanilla ice cream or a dollop of whipped cream on top, if desired.
10. Enjoy this classic Southern dessert with the delicious combination of sweet peaches and buttery cobbler topping!

Molten Chocolate Cake

Ingredients:

- 4 ounces semi-sweet or bittersweet chocolate, chopped
- 1/2 cup (1 stick) unsalted butter
- 1/2 cup granulated sugar
- 2 large eggs
- 2 large egg yolks
- 1 teaspoon vanilla extract
- 1/4 cup all-purpose flour
- Pinch of salt
- Optional: powdered sugar, vanilla ice cream, or whipped cream for serving

Instructions:

1. Preheat your oven to 425°F (220°C). Grease four 6-ounce ramekins or custard cups with butter and dust them lightly with cocoa powder or powdered sugar. Place them on a baking sheet.
2. In a heatproof bowl set over a pot of simmering water (double boiler), melt the chopped chocolate and butter together, stirring until smooth. Remove from heat and let it cool slightly.
3. In a mixing bowl, whisk together the granulated sugar, eggs, egg yolks, and vanilla extract until well combined.
4. Gradually whisk the melted chocolate mixture into the egg mixture until smooth and well combined.
5. Sift the all-purpose flour and salt over the chocolate mixture and gently fold them in until just combined. Be careful not to overmix.
6. Divide the batter evenly among the prepared ramekins, filling each about 3/4 full.
7. Bake in the preheated oven for 12-14 minutes, or until the edges are set but the centers are still soft and slightly jiggly.
8. Remove the molten chocolate cakes from the oven and let them cool in the ramekins for 1-2 minutes.
9. To serve, run a knife around the edges of each ramekin to loosen the cakes. Carefully invert each molten chocolate cake onto a serving plate.
10. Dust with powdered sugar and serve immediately, optionally with a scoop of vanilla ice cream or a dollop of whipped cream on the side.

11. Enjoy these indulgent Molten Chocolate Cakes with their irresistibly gooey centers!

Cinnamon Rolls

Ingredients:

For the dough:

- 1 cup warm milk (110°F-115°F)
- 2 1/4 teaspoons (1 packet) active dry yeast
- 1/2 cup granulated sugar
- 1/3 cup unsalted butter, melted
- 2 large eggs, room temperature
- 4 1/2 cups all-purpose flour
- 1 teaspoon salt

For the filling:

- 1/2 cup unsalted butter, softened
- 1 cup packed brown sugar
- 2 tablespoons ground cinnamon

For the cream cheese icing:

- 4 ounces cream cheese, softened
- 1/4 cup unsalted butter, softened
- 1 cup powdered sugar
- 1/2 teaspoon vanilla extract

Instructions:

1. In a large mixing bowl, combine the warm milk and yeast. Let it sit for 5-10 minutes, or until the yeast is foamy.
2. Add the granulated sugar, melted butter, eggs, flour, and salt to the yeast mixture. Mix until a soft dough forms.
3. Knead the dough on a floured surface for about 5 minutes, or until smooth and elastic. Place the dough in a greased bowl, cover it with a clean kitchen towel or

plastic wrap, and let it rise in a warm place for about 1 hour, or until doubled in size.
4. While the dough is rising, prepare the filling by mixing together the softened butter, brown sugar, and ground cinnamon until well combined. Set aside.
5. Once the dough has doubled in size, punch it down and roll it out on a floured surface into a large rectangle, about 18x14 inches.
6. Spread the cinnamon sugar filling evenly over the dough, leaving a small border around the edges.
7. Starting from one long edge, tightly roll up the dough into a log. Pinch the seam to seal.
8. Use a sharp knife to cut the dough into 12 equal-sized rolls.
9. Place the rolls in a greased 9x13-inch baking dish, leaving a little space between each roll. Cover the dish with a clean kitchen towel or plastic wrap and let the rolls rise in a warm place for another 30-45 minutes, or until puffed up.
10. Preheat your oven to 350°F (175°C). Bake the cinnamon rolls in the preheated oven for 25-30 minutes, or until golden brown.
11. While the rolls are baking, prepare the cream cheese icing by mixing together the softened cream cheese, softened butter, powdered sugar, and vanilla extract until smooth and creamy.
12. Once the cinnamon rolls are done baking, let them cool in the pan for a few minutes before spreading the cream cheese icing over the top.
13. Serve the warm and gooey Homemade Cinnamon Rolls and enjoy the delicious aroma and flavor!

Cheesecake Brownies

Ingredients:

For the brownie layer:

- 1/2 cup (1 stick) unsalted butter
- 1 cup granulated sugar
- 2 large eggs
- 1 teaspoon vanilla extract
- 1/3 cup unsweetened cocoa powder
- 1/2 cup all-purpose flour
- 1/4 teaspoon salt
- 1/4 teaspoon baking powder

For the cheesecake layer:

- 8 ounces cream cheese, softened
- 1/4 cup granulated sugar
- 1 large egg
- 1/2 teaspoon vanilla extract

Instructions:

1. Preheat your oven to 350°F (175°C). Grease or line an 8x8-inch baking pan with parchment paper.
2. For the brownie layer, melt the butter in a medium saucepan over low heat. Remove from heat and stir in the granulated sugar, eggs, and vanilla extract until well combined.
3. In a separate bowl, sift together the cocoa powder, flour, salt, and baking powder. Gradually add the dry ingredients to the wet ingredients, stirring until just combined. Be careful not to overmix.
4. Spread the brownie batter evenly into the prepared baking pan, smoothing the top with a spatula.
5. For the cheesecake layer, in a mixing bowl, beat the softened cream cheese and granulated sugar until smooth and creamy. Add the egg and vanilla extract, and beat until well combined.

6. Pour the cheesecake mixture over the brownie batter in the baking pan, spreading it out evenly with a spatula.
7. Use a knife or skewer to swirl the brownie and cheesecake layers together to create a marbled effect.
8. Bake in the preheated oven for 25-30 minutes, or until the edges are set and a toothpick inserted into the center comes out with a few moist crumbs.
9. Remove the cheesecake brownies from the oven and let them cool completely in the pan on a wire rack.
10. Once cooled, cut the cheesecake brownies into squares and serve. Enjoy the delicious combination of rich chocolate brownie and creamy cheesecake layers!

Pumpkin Pie

Ingredients:

For the pie crust:

- 1 1/4 cups all-purpose flour
- 1/2 teaspoon salt
- 1/2 tablespoon granulated sugar
- 1/2 cup (1 stick) unsalted butter, cold and cut into small cubes
- 3 to 4 tablespoons ice water

For the filling:

- 1 (15-ounce) can pumpkin puree (about 1 3/4 cups)
- 3/4 cup packed light brown sugar
- 2 large eggs
- 1 teaspoon ground cinnamon
- 1/2 teaspoon ground ginger
- 1/4 teaspoon ground nutmeg
- 1/4 teaspoon ground cloves
- 1/4 teaspoon salt
- 1 cup evaporated milk or heavy cream

Instructions:

1. Preheat your oven to 375°F (190°C). Place a baking sheet in the oven to preheat as well.
2. For the pie crust, in a large mixing bowl, whisk together the flour, salt, and granulated sugar. Add the cold cubed butter to the flour mixture.
3. Use a pastry cutter or your fingers to work the butter into the flour mixture until it resembles coarse crumbs and there are some pea-sized pieces of butter remaining.
4. Gradually add the ice water, 1 tablespoon at a time, mixing with a fork until the dough comes together. Be careful not to overwork the dough. If the dough is too dry, add a little more ice water, 1 tablespoon at a time.
5. Shape the dough into a disk, wrap it in plastic wrap, and refrigerate it for at least 30 minutes.

6. On a lightly floured surface, roll out the chilled dough into a circle about 12 inches in diameter. Carefully transfer the dough to a 9-inch pie dish, pressing it gently into the bottom and sides of the dish. Trim any excess dough and crimp the edges as desired.
7. In a large mixing bowl, whisk together the pumpkin puree, packed light brown sugar, eggs, ground cinnamon, ground ginger, ground nutmeg, ground cloves, and salt until smooth and well combined.
8. Gradually add the evaporated milk or heavy cream to the pumpkin mixture, stirring until smooth and well combined.
9. Pour the pumpkin filling into the prepared pie crust, spreading it out evenly with a spatula.
10. Place the pie dish on the preheated baking sheet in the oven. Bake for 50-60 minutes, or until the filling is set and the crust is golden brown.
11. Remove the pumpkin pie from the oven and let it cool completely on a wire rack before slicing and serving.
12. Serve the classic Pumpkin Pie at room temperature or chilled, optionally with a dollop of whipped cream or a scoop of vanilla ice cream on top. Enjoy the warm flavors of fall in every bite!

S'mores Bars

Ingredients:

- 1/2 cup (1 stick) unsalted butter, melted
- 1/4 cup granulated sugar
- 1 large egg
- 1 teaspoon vanilla extract
- 1 1/4 cups graham cracker crumbs
- 1 cup all-purpose flour
- 1/2 teaspoon baking powder
- 1/4 teaspoon salt
- 1 cup chocolate chips
- 2 cups mini marshmallows

Instructions:

1. Preheat your oven to 350°F (175°C). Grease or line a 9x9-inch baking pan with parchment paper.
2. In a large mixing bowl, whisk together the melted butter and granulated sugar until well combined.
3. Add the egg and vanilla extract to the butter mixture, and whisk until smooth.
4. In a separate bowl, combine the graham cracker crumbs, all-purpose flour, baking powder, and salt.
5. Gradually add the dry ingredients to the wet ingredients, stirring until just combined. The mixture will be thick and crumbly.
6. Press about two-thirds of the dough evenly into the bottom of the prepared baking pan, using your hands or a spatula to smooth it out.
7. Sprinkle the chocolate chips evenly over the dough in the pan.
8. Scatter the mini marshmallows over the chocolate chips, covering the entire surface.
9. Crumble the remaining dough evenly over the marshmallows, creating a top layer.
10. Bake in the preheated oven for 20-25 minutes, or until the edges are golden brown and the marshmallows are puffed and lightly toasted.
11. Remove the s'mores bars from the oven and let them cool completely in the pan on a wire rack.
12. Once cooled, use a sharp knife to cut the bars into squares.

13. Serve and enjoy these delicious S'mores Bars with the classic flavors of graham crackers, chocolate, and marshmallows in every bite!

Chocolate Truffles

Ingredients:

- 8 ounces (about 1 1/3 cups) good quality semi-sweet or bittersweet chocolate, chopped
- 1/2 cup heavy cream
- 1 tablespoon unsalted butter, at room temperature
- 1/2 teaspoon vanilla extract
- Optional coatings: cocoa powder, powdered sugar, chopped nuts, shredded coconut, or melted chocolate for dipping

Instructions:

1. Place the chopped chocolate in a heatproof bowl.
2. In a small saucepan, heat the heavy cream over medium heat until it just starts to simmer. Remove from heat immediately.
3. Pour the hot cream over the chopped chocolate. Let it sit for 1-2 minutes to soften the chocolate.
4. Gently stir the chocolate and cream together with a spatula until the chocolate is completely melted and the mixture is smooth and shiny.
5. Add the room temperature butter and vanilla extract to the chocolate mixture. Stir until the butter is melted and fully incorporated.
6. Cover the bowl with plastic wrap and refrigerate the chocolate mixture for at least 2 hours, or until firm enough to handle.
7. Once the chocolate mixture is firm, use a small spoon or a melon baller to scoop out portions of the mixture. Roll each portion between your hands to form a smooth ball. Work quickly to prevent the mixture from melting too much.
8. Roll the truffles in your desired coatings, such as cocoa powder, powdered sugar, chopped nuts, or shredded coconut. Alternatively, you can dip them in melted chocolate for an extra layer of chocolatey goodness.
9. Place the coated truffles on a baking sheet lined with parchment paper.
10. Refrigerate the truffles for about 30 minutes to allow them to firm up.
11. Once firm, transfer the truffles to an airtight container and store them in the refrigerator until ready to serve.
12. Enjoy these decadent and luxurious Chocolate Truffles as a delightful treat or as a homemade gift for someone special!

Cherry Pie

Ingredients:

For the pie crust:

- 2 1/2 cups all-purpose flour
- 1 teaspoon salt
- 1 tablespoon granulated sugar
- 1 cup (2 sticks) unsalted butter, cold and cut into small cubes
- 6-8 tablespoons ice water

For the cherry filling:

- 4 cups fresh or frozen cherries, pitted
- 3/4 cup granulated sugar
- 3 tablespoons cornstarch
- 1 tablespoon lemon juice
- 1/2 teaspoon almond extract
- 1/4 teaspoon salt
- Optional: 1 tablespoon unsalted butter (for dotting the filling)

Instructions:

1. Preheat your oven to 375°F (190°C). Place a baking sheet in the oven to preheat as well.
2. For the pie crust, in a large mixing bowl, whisk together the flour, salt, and granulated sugar. Add the cold cubed butter to the flour mixture.
3. Use a pastry cutter or your fingers to work the butter into the flour mixture until it resembles coarse crumbs and there are some pea-sized pieces of butter remaining.
4. Gradually add the ice water, 1 tablespoon at a time, mixing with a fork until the dough comes together. Be careful not to overwork the dough. If the dough is too dry, add a little more ice water, 1 tablespoon at a time.
5. Divide the dough in half and shape each half into a disk. Wrap each disk in plastic wrap and refrigerate for at least 30 minutes.

6. For the cherry filling, in a large mixing bowl, combine the pitted cherries, granulated sugar, cornstarch, lemon juice, almond extract, and salt. Stir until the cherries are well coated.
7. On a lightly floured surface, roll out one disk of the chilled dough into a circle about 12 inches in diameter. Carefully transfer the dough to a 9-inch pie dish, pressing it gently into the bottom and sides of the dish. Trim any excess dough.
8. Pour the cherry filling into the prepared pie crust, spreading it out evenly.
9. Roll out the second disk of chilled dough into a circle about 12 inches in diameter. Carefully place it over the cherry filling. Trim any excess dough and crimp the edges to seal.
10. Optional: cut slits or create a decorative pattern in the top crust to allow steam to escape during baking.
11. If desired, dot the top of the pie filling with small pieces of unsalted butter.
12. Place the pie dish on the preheated baking sheet in the oven. Bake for 45-55 minutes, or until the crust is golden brown and the filling is bubbly.
13. If the edges of the crust start to brown too quickly, you can cover them with foil halfway through baking.
14. Remove the cherry pie from the oven and let it cool completely on a wire rack before slicing and serving.
15. Serve the classic Cherry Pie at room temperature or slightly warmed, optionally with a scoop of vanilla ice cream or a dollop of whipped cream on top. Enjoy the delicious flavors of sweet cherries in every bite!

Salted Caramel Brownies

Ingredients:

For the brownie layer:

- 1/2 cup (1 stick) unsalted butter
- 1 cup granulated sugar
- 2 large eggs
- 1 teaspoon vanilla extract
- 1/3 cup unsweetened cocoa powder
- 1/2 cup all-purpose flour
- 1/4 teaspoon salt
- 1/4 teaspoon baking powder

For the salted caramel layer:

- 1 cup granulated sugar
- 1/4 cup water
- 1/2 cup heavy cream
- 4 tablespoons unsalted butter
- 1 teaspoon sea salt flakes, plus extra for sprinkling

Instructions:

1. Preheat your oven to 350°F (175°C). Grease or line an 8x8-inch baking pan with parchment paper.
2. For the brownie layer, melt the butter in a medium saucepan over low heat. Remove from heat and stir in the granulated sugar, eggs, and vanilla extract until well combined.
3. In a separate bowl, sift together the cocoa powder, flour, salt, and baking powder. Gradually add the dry ingredients to the wet ingredients, stirring until just combined. Be careful not to overmix.
4. Spread the brownie batter evenly into the prepared baking pan, smoothing the top with a spatula.

5. Bake the brownie layer in the preheated oven for 20-25 minutes, or until the edges are set and a toothpick inserted into the center comes out with a few moist crumbs. Remove from the oven and let it cool slightly.
6. While the brownie layer is cooling, make the salted caramel layer. In a saucepan, combine the granulated sugar and water over medium heat. Stir until the sugar has dissolved.
7. Once the mixture starts boiling, stop stirring and let it cook until it turns a deep amber color, swirling the pan occasionally to ensure even cooking. This will take about 5-7 minutes.
8. Remove the saucepan from heat and carefully pour in the heavy cream. Be cautious as the mixture will bubble vigorously.
9. Stir in the unsalted butter and sea salt flakes until smooth and well combined.
10. Pour the salted caramel over the slightly cooled brownie layer, spreading it out evenly with a spatula.
11. Sprinkle additional sea salt flakes over the top of the caramel layer.
12. Allow the salted caramel brownies to cool completely in the pan on a wire rack.
13. Once cooled, refrigerate the brownies for at least 1 hour to allow the caramel layer to set.
14. Once set, use a sharp knife to cut the brownies into squares.
15. Serve and enjoy these indulgent Salted Caramel Brownies with the perfect balance of sweet and salty flavors!

Apple Pie

Ingredients:

For the pie crust:

- 2 1/2 cups all-purpose flour
- 1 teaspoon salt
- 1 tablespoon granulated sugar
- 1 cup (2 sticks) unsalted butter, cold and cut into small cubes
- 6-8 tablespoons ice water

For the apple filling:

- 6 cups thinly sliced peeled apples (such as Granny Smith, Honeycrisp, or a mix)
- 3/4 cup granulated sugar
- 2 tablespoons all-purpose flour
- 1 teaspoon ground cinnamon
- 1/4 teaspoon ground nutmeg
- 1/4 teaspoon salt
- 1 tablespoon lemon juice
- 1 tablespoon unsalted butter, cut into small pieces

For assembly:

- 1 large egg, beaten (for egg wash)
- 1 tablespoon granulated sugar (for sprinkling)

Instructions:

1. Preheat your oven to 425°F (220°C). Place a baking sheet in the oven to preheat as well.
2. For the pie crust, in a large mixing bowl, whisk together the flour, salt, and granulated sugar. Add the cold cubed butter to the flour mixture.

3. Use a pastry cutter or your fingers to work the butter into the flour mixture until it resembles coarse crumbs and there are some pea-sized pieces of butter remaining.
4. Gradually add the ice water, 1 tablespoon at a time, mixing with a fork until the dough comes together. Be careful not to overwork the dough. If the dough is too dry, add a little more ice water, 1 tablespoon at a time.
5. Divide the dough in half and shape each half into a disk. Wrap each disk in plastic wrap and refrigerate for at least 30 minutes.
6. For the apple filling, in a large mixing bowl, combine the sliced apples, granulated sugar, flour, ground cinnamon, ground nutmeg, salt, and lemon juice. Toss until the apples are well coated.
7. On a lightly floured surface, roll out one disk of the chilled dough into a circle about 12 inches in diameter. Carefully transfer the dough to a 9-inch pie dish, pressing it gently into the bottom and sides of the dish. Trim any excess dough.
8. Pour the apple filling into the prepared pie crust, spreading it out evenly. Dot the top of the filling with small pieces of unsalted butter.
9. Roll out the second disk of chilled dough into a circle about 12 inches in diameter. Carefully place it over the apple filling. Trim any excess dough and crimp the edges to seal.
10. Use a sharp knife to cut slits or create a decorative pattern in the top crust to allow steam to escape during baking.
11. Brush the top crust with the beaten egg and sprinkle with granulated sugar.
12. Place the pie dish on the preheated baking sheet in the oven. Bake for 45-55 minutes, or until the crust is golden brown and the filling is bubbly.
13. If the edges of the crust start to brown too quickly, you can cover them with foil halfway through baking.
14. Remove the apple pie from the oven and let it cool completely on a wire rack before slicing and serving.
15. Serve the classic Apple Pie at room temperature or slightly warmed, optionally with a scoop of vanilla ice cream or a dollop of whipped cream on top. Enjoy the delicious flavors of tender apples and warm spices in every bite!

Rice Krispie Treats

Ingredients:

- 6 cups Rice Krispies cereal (or similar crisp rice cereal)
- 1/4 cup (1/2 stick) unsalted butter
- 1 package (10 ounces) marshmallows (about 40 regular-sized marshmallows)
- Optional: 1/2 teaspoon vanilla extract

Instructions:

1. Grease a 9x13-inch baking dish or line it with parchment paper. Set aside.
2. In a large pot, melt the butter over low heat.
3. Once the butter is melted, add the marshmallows to the pot. Stir constantly until the marshmallows are completely melted and smooth. If using vanilla extract, stir it in at this point.
4. Remove the pot from the heat. Quickly add the Rice Krispies cereal to the melted marshmallow mixture. Stir until the cereal is evenly coated with the marshmallow mixture.
5. Transfer the mixture to the prepared baking dish. Use a buttered spatula or wax paper to press the mixture firmly and evenly into the dish.
6. Allow the Rice Krispie treats to cool and set at room temperature for about 30 minutes to an hour.
7. Once set, use a sharp knife to cut the treats into squares or rectangles.
8. Serve and enjoy these classic Rice Krispie Treats as a delicious snack or dessert!

Variations:

- Chocolate Rice Krispie Treats: Add 1/2 cup of semi-sweet chocolate chips to the melted marshmallow mixture and stir until melted and smooth before adding the cereal.
- Peanut Butter Rice Krispie Treats: Add 1/2 cup of creamy peanut butter to the melted marshmallow mixture and stir until smooth before adding the cereal.
- Sprinkle Rice Krispie Treats: Add colorful sprinkles on top of the treats after pressing them into the baking dish for a festive touch.

- Chocolate Drizzled Rice Krispie Treats: Melt some chocolate chips and drizzle it over the cooled and cut Rice Krispie Treats for an extra chocolatey finish.

Chocolate Covered Pretzels

Ingredients:

- 1 bag (about 12 ounces) of pretzels (mini pretzels, twists, or rods)
- 8 ounces of chocolate (semi-sweet, milk, or white chocolate), chopped
- Optional toppings: sprinkles, chopped nuts, crushed candies, shredded coconut, sea salt, etc.

Instructions:

1. Line a baking sheet with parchment paper or wax paper. Set aside.
2. In a heatproof bowl, melt the chocolate in the microwave in 30-second intervals, stirring after each interval, until smooth. Alternatively, you can melt the chocolate using a double boiler on the stove.
3. Once the chocolate is melted and smooth, dip each pretzel into the chocolate, coating it halfway or fully, depending on your preference. Use a fork or dipping tool to help coat the pretzels evenly and shake off any excess chocolate.
4. Place the chocolate-covered pretzels on the prepared baking sheet, spacing them out slightly.
5. If desired, sprinkle your chosen toppings over the chocolate-covered pretzels before the chocolate sets. You can also drizzle additional melted chocolate over the pretzels for a decorative touch.
6. Allow the chocolate-covered pretzels to set at room temperature until the chocolate hardens, or you can speed up the process by placing the baking sheet in the refrigerator for about 15-20 minutes.
7. Once the chocolate has set and hardened, transfer the chocolate-covered pretzels to an airtight container for storage.
8. Serve and enjoy these delicious Chocolate Covered Pretzels as a sweet and salty snack or as a fun treat for parties and gatherings!

Lemon Meringue Pie

Ingredients:

For the crust:

- 1 1/4 cups all-purpose flour
- 1/2 teaspoon salt
- 1/2 cup (1 stick) unsalted butter, chilled and cubed
- 3-4 tablespoons ice water

For the lemon filling:

- 1 cup granulated sugar
- 1/4 cup cornstarch
- 1/4 teaspoon salt
- 1 1/2 cups water
- 4 large egg yolks
- 1 tablespoon lemon zest
- 1/2 cup fresh lemon juice (about 3-4 lemons)
- 2 tablespoons unsalted butter

For the meringue topping:

- 4 large egg whites, at room temperature
- 1/2 teaspoon cream of tartar
- 1/2 cup granulated sugar
- 1/2 teaspoon vanilla extract

Instructions:

1. Preheat your oven to 375°F (190°C). Place a baking sheet in the oven to preheat as well.
2. For the crust, in a large mixing bowl, whisk together the flour and salt. Add the chilled cubed butter to the flour mixture.
3. Use a pastry cutter or your fingers to work the butter into the flour mixture until it resembles coarse crumbs and there are some pea-sized pieces of butter remaining.

4. Gradually add the ice water, 1 tablespoon at a time, mixing with a fork until the dough comes together. Be careful not to overwork the dough. If the dough is too dry, add a little more ice water, 1 tablespoon at a time.
5. Shape the dough into a disk, wrap it in plastic wrap, and refrigerate it for at least 30 minutes.
6. On a lightly floured surface, roll out the chilled dough into a circle about 12 inches in diameter. Carefully transfer the dough to a 9-inch pie dish, pressing it gently into the bottom and sides of the dish. Trim any excess dough and crimp the edges as desired. Prick the bottom of the crust with a fork.
7. Line the crust with parchment paper or aluminum foil, and fill it with pie weights or dried beans. Bake in the preheated oven for 15 minutes. Remove the parchment paper and weights, and bake for an additional 10-15 minutes, or until the crust is golden brown. Remove from the oven and let it cool completely.
8. For the lemon filling, in a medium saucepan, whisk together the granulated sugar, cornstarch, and salt. Gradually whisk in the water until smooth. Cook over medium heat, stirring constantly, until the mixture comes to a boil and thickens.
9. In a separate bowl, whisk the egg yolks until smooth. Gradually whisk in about 1/2 cup of the hot sugar mixture to temper the eggs, then pour the egg mixture back into the saucepan, whisking constantly.
10. Cook the mixture over medium heat, stirring constantly, for an additional 2-3 minutes, or until thickened.
11. Remove the saucepan from the heat and stir in the lemon zest, lemon juice, and unsalted butter until smooth. Pour the lemon filling into the cooled pie crust.
12. For the meringue topping, in a clean mixing bowl, beat the egg whites and cream of tartar on high speed until soft peaks form. Gradually add the granulated sugar, 1 tablespoon at a time, beating until stiff peaks form. Beat in the vanilla extract.
13. Spread the meringue over the hot lemon filling, making sure to spread it all the way to the edges of the crust to seal it in.
14. Use the back of a spoon to create peaks and swirls in the meringue.
15. Bake the pie in the preheated oven for 10-12 minutes, or until the meringue is lightly browned.
16. Remove the pie from the oven and let it cool completely on a wire rack.
17. Once cooled, refrigerate the lemon meringue pie for at least 4 hours, or until set.
18. Serve and enjoy this classic Lemon Meringue Pie with its tangy lemon filling and fluffy meringue topping!

Black Forest Cake

Ingredients:

For the chocolate cake layers:

- 2 cups all-purpose flour
- 3/4 cup unsweetened cocoa powder
- 2 cups granulated sugar
- 2 teaspoons baking powder
- 1 1/2 teaspoons baking soda
- 1 teaspoon salt
- 2 large eggs
- 1 cup milk
- 1/2 cup vegetable oil
- 2 teaspoons vanilla extract
- 1 cup boiling water

For the cherry filling:

- 1 (21-ounce) can cherry pie filling

For the whipped cream frosting:

- 3 cups heavy cream, chilled
- 1/2 cup powdered sugar
- 1 teaspoon vanilla extract

For garnish:

- Chocolate shavings or curls
- Maraschino cherries

Instructions:

1. Preheat your oven to 350°F (175°C). Grease and flour three 9-inch round cake pans. Line the bottoms with parchment paper for easy removal.

2. In a large mixing bowl, sift together the flour, cocoa powder, granulated sugar, baking powder, baking soda, and salt.
3. Add the eggs, milk, vegetable oil, and vanilla extract to the dry ingredients. Beat on medium speed for 2 minutes.
4. Stir in the boiling water until the batter is well combined. The batter will be thin.
5. Divide the batter evenly among the prepared cake pans.
6. Bake in the preheated oven for 30-35 minutes, or until a toothpick inserted into the center of the cakes comes out clean.
7. Remove the cakes from the oven and let them cool in the pans for 10 minutes before transferring them to wire racks to cool completely.
8. Once the cakes have cooled completely, level the tops of the cakes using a serrated knife if necessary.
9. To assemble the cake, place one cake layer on a serving plate or cake stand. Spread a layer of cherry pie filling over the top of the cake layer.
10. In a mixing bowl, whip the chilled heavy cream, powdered sugar, and vanilla extract until stiff peaks form.
11. Spread a layer of whipped cream over the cherry filling.
12. Repeat with the remaining cake layers, cherry filling, and whipped cream.
13. Frost the top and sides of the cake with the remaining whipped cream.
14. Garnish the top of the cake with chocolate shavings or curls and maraschino cherries.
15. Refrigerate the Black Forest Cake for at least 1 hour before serving to allow the flavors to meld together.
16. Serve and enjoy this delicious and classic Black Forest Cake with its layers of moist chocolate cake, cherry filling, and fluffy whipped cream frosting!

Peanut Butter Cookies

Ingredients:

- 1/2 cup (1 stick) unsalted butter, softened
- 1/2 cup creamy peanut butter
- 1/2 cup granulated sugar, plus extra for rolling
- 1/2 cup packed light brown sugar
- 1 large egg
- 1 teaspoon vanilla extract
- 1 1/4 cups all-purpose flour
- 1/2 teaspoon baking powder
- 1/2 teaspoon baking soda
- 1/4 teaspoon salt

Instructions:

1. Preheat your oven to 350°F (175°C). Line baking sheets with parchment paper or silicone baking mats. Set aside.
2. In a large mixing bowl, cream together the softened butter, creamy peanut butter, granulated sugar, and brown sugar until light and fluffy.
3. Add the egg and vanilla extract to the peanut butter mixture, and beat until well combined.
4. In a separate bowl, whisk together the all-purpose flour, baking powder, baking soda, and salt.
5. Gradually add the dry ingredients to the wet ingredients, mixing until just combined. Be careful not to overmix.
6. Scoop out tablespoon-sized portions of dough and roll them into balls.
7. Roll each dough ball in granulated sugar to coat evenly.
8. Place the coated dough balls on the prepared baking sheets, spacing them about 2 inches apart.
9. Use a fork to flatten each dough ball slightly and create a crisscross pattern on top.
10. Bake in the preheated oven for 10-12 minutes, or until the cookies are lightly golden brown around the edges.
11. Remove the cookies from the oven and let them cool on the baking sheets for 5 minutes before transferring them to wire racks to cool completely.

12. Once cooled, store the peanut butter cookies in an airtight container at room temperature for up to one week.
13. Serve and enjoy these classic Peanut Butter Cookies as a delicious treat any time of day!

Chocolate Pudding

Ingredients:

- 1/2 cup granulated sugar
- 1/4 cup unsweetened cocoa powder
- 1/4 cup cornstarch
- 1/8 teaspoon salt
- 2 3/4 cups whole milk
- 2 large egg yolks
- 2 tablespoons unsalted butter
- 1 teaspoon vanilla extract

Instructions:

1. In a medium saucepan, whisk together the granulated sugar, cocoa powder, cornstarch, and salt until well combined.
2. Gradually whisk in the whole milk until smooth and no lumps remain.
3. Place the saucepan over medium heat and cook, stirring constantly, until the mixture thickens and comes to a boil. This will take about 8-10 minutes.
4. Once the mixture boils, continue to cook and stir for an additional 1-2 minutes until it is very thick.
5. In a small bowl, whisk the egg yolks until smooth. Gradually whisk in about 1/2 cup of the hot pudding mixture to temper the eggs.
6. Pour the tempered egg mixture back into the saucepan with the remaining pudding mixture, whisking constantly.
7. Cook the pudding mixture, stirring constantly, for an additional 1-2 minutes until it thickens even more.
8. Remove the saucepan from the heat and stir in the unsalted butter and vanilla extract until the butter is melted and the mixture is smooth.
9. Strain the pudding through a fine-mesh sieve into a clean bowl to remove any lumps or bits of cooked egg.
10. Divide the pudding among serving dishes or pour it into a large serving bowl.
11. Place plastic wrap directly on the surface of the pudding to prevent a skin from forming.
12. Refrigerate the pudding for at least 2-3 hours, or until chilled and set.

13. Serve the homemade chocolate pudding chilled, optionally topped with whipped cream or chocolate shavings.
14. Enjoy this rich and creamy Chocolate Pudding as a delicious dessert or snack!

Strawberry Rhubarb Crisp

Ingredients:

For the filling:

- 3 cups chopped rhubarb (about 1/2-inch pieces)
- 3 cups sliced strawberries
- 1/2 cup granulated sugar
- 1/4 cup cornstarch
- 1 tablespoon fresh lemon juice
- 1 teaspoon vanilla extract

For the crisp topping:

- 1 cup old-fashioned rolled oats
- 1/2 cup all-purpose flour
- 1/2 cup packed light brown sugar
- 1/2 teaspoon ground cinnamon
- 1/4 teaspoon salt
- 1/2 cup (1 stick) unsalted butter, cold and cut into small cubes

Instructions:

1. Preheat your oven to 375°F (190°C). Grease a 9x9-inch baking dish or a similar-sized baking dish. Set aside.
2. In a large mixing bowl, combine the chopped rhubarb, sliced strawberries, granulated sugar, cornstarch, lemon juice, and vanilla extract. Toss until the fruit is well coated.
3. Transfer the fruit mixture to the prepared baking dish, spreading it out evenly.
4. In a separate mixing bowl, combine the rolled oats, all-purpose flour, light brown sugar, ground cinnamon, and salt.
5. Add the cold cubed butter to the oat mixture. Use a pastry cutter or your fingers to work the butter into the dry ingredients until the mixture resembles coarse crumbs and there are some pea-sized pieces of butter remaining.
6. Sprinkle the crisp topping evenly over the fruit mixture in the baking dish.
7. Bake in the preheated oven for 35-40 minutes, or until the fruit is bubbling and the topping is golden brown and crisp.

8. Remove the crisp from the oven and let it cool slightly before serving.
9. Serve the Strawberry Rhubarb Crisp warm or at room temperature, optionally topped with vanilla ice cream or whipped cream.
10. Enjoy this delightful dessert that combines the tartness of rhubarb with the sweetness of strawberries, all topped with a crispy oat topping!

Mint Chocolate Chip Ice Cream

Ingredients:

- 2 cups heavy cream
- 1 cup whole milk
- 3/4 cup granulated sugar
- Pinch of salt
- 1 teaspoon pure vanilla extract
- 1 teaspoon peppermint extract
- Green food coloring (optional)
- 3/4 cup semi-sweet chocolate chips or chopped chocolate

Instructions:

1. In a mixing bowl, whisk together the heavy cream, whole milk, granulated sugar, salt, vanilla extract, and peppermint extract until the sugar is dissolved.
2. If desired, add a few drops of green food coloring to achieve the desired mint color. Mix until well combined.
3. Pour the mixture into the bowl of an ice cream maker and churn according to the manufacturer's instructions, usually for about 20-25 minutes, or until the mixture reaches a soft-serve consistency.
4. During the last few minutes of churning, add the semi-sweet chocolate chips or chopped chocolate into the ice cream maker, allowing them to mix evenly into the ice cream.
5. Once the ice cream has reached the desired consistency and the chocolate chips are evenly distributed, transfer the ice cream to a freezer-safe container.
6. Cover the container with a lid or plastic wrap, ensuring it touches the surface of the ice cream to prevent ice crystals from forming.
7. Freeze the ice cream for at least 4 hours, or until firm.
8. Before serving, let the ice cream sit at room temperature for a few minutes to soften slightly for easier scooping.
9. Scoop the Mint Chocolate Chip Ice Cream into bowls or cones, and enjoy this refreshing and creamy treat with bursts of chocolate throughout!

Blondies

Ingredients:

- 1 cup (2 sticks) unsalted butter, melted
- 2 cups packed light brown sugar
- 2 large eggs
- 1 tablespoon vanilla extract
- 2 cups all-purpose flour
- 1 teaspoon baking powder
- 1/2 teaspoon salt
- Optional add-ins: chocolate chips, chopped nuts, butterscotch chips, white chocolate chips, etc.

Instructions:

1. Preheat your oven to 350°F (175°C). Grease or line a 9x13-inch baking pan with parchment paper. Set aside.
2. In a large mixing bowl, whisk together the melted butter and packed light brown sugar until well combined.
3. Add the eggs and vanilla extract to the butter-sugar mixture, and whisk until smooth and creamy.
4. In a separate bowl, sift together the all-purpose flour, baking powder, and salt.
5. Gradually add the dry ingredients to the wet ingredients, stirring until just combined. Be careful not to overmix.
6. If desired, fold in any optional add-ins, such as chocolate chips or chopped nuts, until evenly distributed throughout the batter.
7. Spread the blondie batter evenly into the prepared baking pan, smoothing the top with a spatula.
8. Bake in the preheated oven for 25-30 minutes, or until the blondies are golden brown and a toothpick inserted into the center comes out with a few moist crumbs.
9. Remove the blondies from the oven and let them cool completely in the pan on a wire rack.
10. Once cooled, use a sharp knife to cut the blondies into squares or rectangles.
11. Serve and enjoy these delicious and chewy Blondies as a delightful treat for any occasion!

Raspberry Tart

Ingredients:

For the crust:

- 1 1/4 cups all-purpose flour
- 1/4 cup granulated sugar
- 1/2 cup (1 stick) unsalted butter, cold and cut into small cubes
- 1 large egg yolk
- 1-2 tablespoons ice water

For the filling:

- 3 cups fresh raspberries
- 1/4 cup granulated sugar
- 1 tablespoon cornstarch
- 1 tablespoon fresh lemon juice

For garnish (optional):

- Powdered sugar
- Fresh mint leaves

Instructions:

1. Preheat your oven to 375°F (190°C). Grease a 9-inch tart pan with a removable bottom. Set aside.
2. In a food processor, combine the all-purpose flour and granulated sugar. Add the cold cubed butter and pulse until the mixture resembles coarse crumbs.
3. Add the egg yolk and 1 tablespoon of ice water to the mixture. Pulse until the dough starts to come together. If the dough is too dry, add another tablespoon of ice water and pulse again.
4. Transfer the dough to a lightly floured surface and gently knead it a few times until it forms a smooth ball.

5. Roll out the dough into a circle large enough to fit into the prepared tart pan. Carefully transfer the dough to the tart pan, pressing it gently into the bottom and sides of the pan. Trim any excess dough.
6. Prick the bottom of the crust with a fork. Place a piece of parchment paper or aluminum foil over the crust and fill it with pie weights or dried beans.
7. Bake the crust in the preheated oven for 15 minutes. Remove the parchment paper and weights, and bake for an additional 5-10 minutes, or until the crust is golden brown. Remove from the oven and let it cool completely.
8. In a medium saucepan, combine the fresh raspberries, granulated sugar, cornstarch, and fresh lemon juice. Cook over medium heat, stirring gently, until the raspberries release their juices and the mixture thickens slightly, about 5-7 minutes. Remove from heat and let it cool slightly.
9. Pour the raspberry filling into the cooled tart crust, spreading it out evenly.
10. Refrigerate the raspberry tart for at least 1-2 hours, or until the filling is set.
11. Before serving, garnish the raspberry tart with powdered sugar and fresh mint leaves, if desired.
12. Slice and serve this delicious Raspberry Tart as a delightful dessert for any occasion!

Chocolate Eclairs

Ingredients:

For the pastry dough (pâte à choux):

- 1/2 cup water
- 1/2 cup whole milk
- 1/2 cup (1 stick) unsalted butter, cut into small pieces
- 1 tablespoon granulated sugar
- 1/4 teaspoon salt
- 1 cup all-purpose flour
- 4 large eggs

For the filling:

- 1 1/2 cups whole milk
- 1/3 cup granulated sugar
- Pinch of salt
- 4 large egg yolks
- 1/4 cup cornstarch
- 1 teaspoon vanilla extract
- 1 cup heavy cream, whipped (for Chantilly cream)

For the chocolate glaze:

- 1/2 cup heavy cream
- 4 ounces semi-sweet chocolate, chopped
- 1 tablespoon unsalted butter

Instructions:

1. Preheat your oven to 425°F (220°C). Line a baking sheet with parchment paper or a silicone baking mat. Set aside.
2. In a medium saucepan, combine the water, milk, butter, sugar, and salt. Heat over medium heat until the mixture comes to a simmer and the butter is melted.

3. Reduce the heat to low, and add the flour all at once. Stir vigorously with a wooden spoon until the mixture forms a smooth ball and pulls away from the sides of the pan, about 1-2 minutes.
4. Transfer the dough to a mixing bowl and let it cool slightly for about 5 minutes.
5. Add the eggs one at a time, mixing well after each addition, until the dough is smooth and glossy.
6. Transfer the dough to a piping bag fitted with a large round tip (or simply cut the corner off a resealable plastic bag).
7. Pipe the dough onto the prepared baking sheet into oblong shapes, about 4 inches long and 1 inch wide, leaving space between each éclair.
8. Bake in the preheated oven for 15 minutes, then reduce the oven temperature to 375°F (190°C) and continue baking for an additional 20-25 minutes, or until the éclairs are puffed, golden brown, and crisp.
9. Remove the éclairs from the oven and transfer them to a wire rack to cool completely.
10. While the éclairs are cooling, prepare the filling. In a medium saucepan, heat the milk, sugar, and salt over medium heat until steaming, but not boiling.
11. In a separate bowl, whisk together the egg yolks and cornstarch until smooth. Gradually whisk in the hot milk mixture.
12. Return the mixture to the saucepan and cook over medium heat, stirring constantly, until thickened, about 5-7 minutes.
13. Remove the pastry cream from the heat and stir in the vanilla extract. Transfer the pastry cream to a bowl and cover it with plastic wrap, pressing the plastic wrap directly onto the surface of the pastry cream to prevent a skin from forming. Refrigerate until chilled.
14. Once the pastry cream is chilled, fold in the whipped cream to make Chantilly cream.
15. Cut the éclairs in half horizontally using a serrated knife. Fill each éclair with the Chantilly cream using a piping bag fitted with a small round tip or a spoon.
16. To make the chocolate glaze, heat the heavy cream in a small saucepan until simmering. Remove from heat and add the chopped chocolate and butter. Let it sit for a minute, then stir until smooth and glossy.
17. Dip the tops of the filled éclairs into the chocolate glaze, allowing any excess glaze to drip off.
18. Place the glazed éclairs on a wire rack to set for a few minutes before serving.
19. Serve and enjoy these delicious Chocolate Éclairs as a delightful dessert or treat!

Apple Turnovers

Ingredients:

For the filling:

- 3 cups peeled, cored, and diced apples (about 3-4 medium-sized apples)
- 1/4 cup granulated sugar
- 2 tablespoons all-purpose flour
- 1 teaspoon ground cinnamon
- 1/4 teaspoon ground nutmeg
- Pinch of salt
- 1 tablespoon lemon juice
- 1 tablespoon unsalted butter

For the pastry:

- 2 sheets store-bought puff pastry, thawed according to package instructions
- 1 large egg, beaten (for egg wash)
- 1 tablespoon granulated sugar (for sprinkling)

Instructions:

1. Preheat your oven to 400°F (200°C). Line a baking sheet with parchment paper or silicone baking mat. Set aside.
2. In a medium saucepan, combine the diced apples, granulated sugar, all-purpose flour, ground cinnamon, ground nutmeg, salt, and lemon juice. Cook over medium heat, stirring occasionally, until the apples are tender and the mixture is thickened, about 5-7 minutes. Remove from heat and stir in the unsalted butter until melted. Let the filling cool slightly.
3. On a lightly floured surface, roll out one sheet of puff pastry into a square or rectangle, about 1/8-inch thick. Use a sharp knife or pastry cutter to cut the pastry into 4 equal squares or rectangles.
4. Place a spoonful of the cooled apple filling onto one half of each pastry square or rectangle, leaving a border around the edges.
5. Fold the other half of the pastry over the filling to create a triangle or rectangle shape. Use a fork to crimp the edges of the turnovers to seal them.

6. Transfer the turnovers to the prepared baking sheet, spacing them a few inches apart.
7. Repeat the process with the remaining sheet of puff pastry and apple filling.
8. Brush the tops of the turnovers with beaten egg wash and sprinkle with granulated sugar.
9. Use a sharp knife to make a few small slits in the tops of the turnovers to allow steam to escape during baking.
10. Bake in the preheated oven for 20-25 minutes, or until the turnovers are golden brown and puffed up.
11. Remove from the oven and let the turnovers cool slightly on the baking sheet before transferring them to a wire rack to cool completely.
12. Serve the apple turnovers warm or at room temperature, optionally dusted with powdered sugar or served with a scoop of vanilla ice cream.
13. Enjoy these delicious Apple Turnovers as a delightful dessert or snack!

Caramel Popcorn

Ingredients:

- 12 cups popped popcorn (about 1/2 cup unpopped kernels)
- 1 cup unsalted butter
- 2 cups packed brown sugar
- 1/2 cup light corn syrup
- 1 teaspoon salt
- 1/2 teaspoon baking soda
- 1 teaspoon vanilla extract

Instructions:

1. Preheat your oven to 250°F (120°C). Line a large baking sheet with parchment paper or a silicone baking mat. Set aside.
2. Place the popped popcorn in a large mixing bowl, removing any unpopped kernels. Set aside.
3. In a medium saucepan, melt the unsalted butter over medium heat. Stir in the packed brown sugar, light corn syrup, and salt until well combined.
4. Bring the mixture to a boil, stirring constantly. Once boiling, stop stirring and let the mixture boil for 4-5 minutes without stirring.
5. Remove the saucepan from the heat and stir in the baking soda and vanilla extract. The mixture will bubble up, so be careful.
6. Pour the hot caramel sauce over the popped popcorn in the mixing bowl. Use a spatula or wooden spoon to gently toss the popcorn until evenly coated with the caramel sauce.
7. Spread the caramel-coated popcorn in an even layer on the prepared baking sheet.
8. Bake in the preheated oven for 45-60 minutes, stirring every 15 minutes, until the caramel popcorn is crispy and no longer sticky.
9. Remove the baking sheet from the oven and let the caramel popcorn cool completely on the baking sheet.
10. Once cooled, break the caramel popcorn into clusters and store it in an airtight container or resealable bags.
11. Enjoy this homemade Caramel Popcorn as a delicious sweet treat for movie nights, parties, or anytime snacking!

Lemon Poppy Seed Cake

Ingredients:

For the cake:

- 2 cups all-purpose flour
- 2 tablespoons poppy seeds
- 1 teaspoon baking powder
- 1/2 teaspoon baking soda
- 1/4 teaspoon salt
- 1 cup unsalted butter, softened
- 1 1/2 cups granulated sugar
- 4 large eggs
- 1/4 cup lemon juice
- Zest of 2 lemons
- 1/2 cup sour cream
- 1 teaspoon vanilla extract

For the glaze:

- 1 cup powdered sugar
- 2-3 tablespoons lemon juice

Instructions:

1. Preheat your oven to 350°F (175°C). Grease and flour a 9x5-inch loaf pan. Set aside.
2. In a medium bowl, whisk together the all-purpose flour, poppy seeds, baking powder, baking soda, and salt. Set aside.
3. In a large mixing bowl, cream together the softened unsalted butter and granulated sugar until light and fluffy.
4. Add the eggs one at a time, beating well after each addition.
5. Stir in the lemon juice and lemon zest until well combined.
6. Gradually add the dry ingredients to the wet ingredients, alternating with the sour cream, beginning and ending with the dry ingredients. Mix until just combined. Do not overmix.

7. Stir in the vanilla extract until evenly distributed throughout the batter.
8. Pour the batter into the prepared loaf pan and smooth the top with a spatula.
9. Bake in the preheated oven for 50-60 minutes, or until a toothpick inserted into the center of the cake comes out clean.
10. Remove the cake from the oven and let it cool in the pan for 10 minutes before transferring it to a wire rack to cool completely.
11. While the cake is cooling, prepare the glaze. In a small bowl, whisk together the powdered sugar and lemon juice until smooth. Adjust the consistency by adding more lemon juice if too thick or more powdered sugar if too thin.
12. Once the cake has cooled completely, drizzle the glaze over the top of the cake.
13. Allow the glaze to set for a few minutes before slicing and serving.
14. Serve and enjoy this delightful Lemon Poppy Seed Cake as a delicious dessert or snack with a cup of tea or coffee!

Almond Biscotti

Ingredients:

- 2 cups all-purpose flour
- 1 cup granulated sugar
- 1 teaspoon baking powder
- 1/4 teaspoon salt
- 3 large eggs
- 1 teaspoon vanilla extract
- 1/2 teaspoon almond extract
- 1 cup almonds, chopped or sliced
- Optional: 1/2 cup chocolate chips or chopped chocolate (for dipping)

Instructions:

1. Preheat your oven to 350°F (175°C). Line a baking sheet with parchment paper or a silicone baking mat. Set aside.
2. In a large mixing bowl, whisk together the all-purpose flour, granulated sugar, baking powder, and salt.
3. In a separate bowl, beat the eggs with the vanilla extract and almond extract until well combined.
4. Pour the egg mixture into the dry ingredients and mix until a dough forms. Fold in the chopped almonds until evenly distributed throughout the dough.
5. Divide the dough in half. On a lightly floured surface, shape each half into a log about 12 inches long and 2 inches wide. Place the logs on the prepared baking sheet, spacing them a few inches apart.
6. Bake in the preheated oven for 25-30 minutes, or until the logs are lightly golden brown and firm to the touch.
7. Remove the baking sheet from the oven and let the logs cool on the baking sheet for 10 minutes.
8. Using a serrated knife, carefully slice the logs diagonally into 1/2-inch thick slices.
9. Arrange the sliced biscotti cut-side down on the baking sheet and return them to the oven.
10. Bake for an additional 10-15 minutes, or until the biscotti are golden brown and crisp. Remove from the oven and let them cool completely on the baking sheet.

11. Optional: Once the biscotti are cooled, melt the chocolate chips or chopped chocolate in the microwave or over a double boiler. Dip one end of each biscotti into the melted chocolate and place them on a wire rack to set.
12. Once the chocolate has set, serve and enjoy these delicious Almond Biscotti with a cup of coffee or tea!

Note: Store the biscotti in an airtight container at room temperature for up to two weeks. They also freeze well for longer storage.

Raspberry Chocolate Chip Cookies

Ingredients:

- 1/2 cup unsalted butter, softened
- 1/2 cup granulated sugar
- 1/2 cup packed light brown sugar
- 1 large egg
- 1 teaspoon vanilla extract
- 1 1/2 cups all-purpose flour
- 1/2 teaspoon baking soda
- 1/4 teaspoon salt
- 1 cup semi-sweet chocolate chips
- 1/2 cup fresh raspberries, washed and dried

Instructions:

1. Preheat your oven to 350°F (175°C). Line a baking sheet with parchment paper or a silicone baking mat. Set aside.
2. In a large mixing bowl, cream together the softened unsalted butter, granulated sugar, and packed light brown sugar until light and fluffy.
3. Add the egg and vanilla extract to the butter-sugar mixture, and beat until well combined.
4. In a separate bowl, whisk together the all-purpose flour, baking soda, and salt.
5. Gradually add the dry ingredients to the wet ingredients, mixing until just combined.
6. Fold in the semi-sweet chocolate chips until evenly distributed throughout the cookie dough.
7. Gently fold in the fresh raspberries, being careful not to crush them too much.
8. Use a cookie scoop or tablespoon to drop rounded dough onto the prepared baking sheet, spacing them about 2 inches apart.
9. Bake in the preheated oven for 10-12 minutes, or until the edges are lightly golden brown.
10. Remove the baking sheet from the oven and let the cookies cool on the baking sheet for 5 minutes before transferring them to a wire rack to cool completely.
11. Serve and enjoy these delicious Raspberry Chocolate Chip Cookies with a glass of milk or cup of coffee!

Chocolate Covered Bananas

Ingredients:

- 4 ripe bananas, peeled and cut into halves
- 8 popsicle sticks or wooden skewers
- 8 ounces semi-sweet chocolate, chopped
- 2 tablespoons coconut oil or vegetable oil
- Toppings of your choice: chopped nuts, shredded coconut, sprinkles, crushed cookies, etc.

Instructions:

1. Insert a popsicle stick or wooden skewer into each banana half, about halfway through. Place the bananas on a parchment-lined baking sheet and freeze them for at least 1 hour, or until firm.
2. In a microwave-safe bowl, combine the chopped semi-sweet chocolate and coconut oil. Microwave in 30-second intervals, stirring between each interval, until the chocolate is melted and smooth.
3. Remove the frozen banana halves from the freezer. Working quickly, dip each banana half into the melted chocolate, using a spoon or spatula to coat it evenly.
4. Allow any excess chocolate to drip off, then place the chocolate-covered bananas back onto the parchment-lined baking sheet.
5. While the chocolate is still wet, sprinkle your desired toppings over the bananas, pressing them gently into the chocolate to adhere.
6. Once all the bananas are coated and decorated, return the baking sheet to the freezer and freeze the bananas until the chocolate is firm, about 30 minutes to 1 hour.
7. Once the chocolate is firm, transfer the chocolate-covered bananas to an airtight container or resealable plastic bag for storage in the freezer.
8. Serve the chocolate-covered bananas straight from the freezer as a refreshing and indulgent treat!

Enjoy these delicious Chocolate Covered Bananas as a healthy and satisfying dessert option!

Coconut Cream Pie

Ingredients:

For the crust:

- 1 1/4 cups all-purpose flour
- 1/2 teaspoon salt
- 1/2 cup (1 stick) unsalted butter, chilled and cut into small pieces
- 2-4 tablespoons ice water

For the filling:

- 1 cup sweetened shredded coconut
- 2 cups whole milk
- 1 cup canned coconut milk
- 3/4 cup granulated sugar
- 1/4 cup cornstarch
- 4 large egg yolks
- 1 teaspoon vanilla extract
- 1/4 teaspoon coconut extract (optional)
- 2 tablespoons unsalted butter

For the topping:

- 1 1/2 cups heavy cream
- 2 tablespoons powdered sugar
- 1/2 teaspoon vanilla extract
- Toasted coconut flakes, for garnish (optional)

Instructions:

1. To make the crust, in a food processor, combine the all-purpose flour and salt. Add the chilled butter pieces and pulse until the mixture resembles coarse crumbs.

2. Gradually add the ice water, 1 tablespoon at a time, and pulse until the dough comes together and forms a ball. Be careful not to overmix.
3. Flatten the dough into a disk, wrap it in plastic wrap, and refrigerate for at least 1 hour.
4. Preheat your oven to 375°F (190°C). Roll out the chilled dough on a lightly floured surface into a circle large enough to fit into a 9-inch pie dish. Transfer the dough to the pie dish and trim any excess. Crimp the edges decoratively.
5. Line the pie crust with parchment paper or aluminum foil and fill it with pie weights or dried beans. Bake in the preheated oven for 15 minutes. Remove the weights and parchment paper, and bake for an additional 10-15 minutes, or until the crust is golden brown. Let it cool completely.
6. To make the filling, spread the sweetened shredded coconut on a baking sheet and toast it in the oven at 350°F (175°C) for 5-7 minutes, or until lightly golden brown. Set aside.
7. In a saucepan, combine the whole milk, canned coconut milk, granulated sugar, and cornstarch. Cook over medium heat, stirring constantly, until the mixture thickens and comes to a simmer.
8. In a separate bowl, whisk the egg yolks. Gradually whisk in about 1/2 cup of the hot milk mixture to temper the eggs. Then, pour the egg mixture back into the saucepan with the remaining milk mixture, whisking constantly.
9. Cook the filling mixture, stirring constantly, for an additional 2-3 minutes, or until thickened.
10. Remove the saucepan from the heat and stir in the vanilla extract, coconut extract (if using), toasted coconut, and unsalted butter until smooth.
11. Pour the filling into the cooled pie crust and smooth the top with a spatula. Refrigerate the pie for at least 4 hours, or until chilled and set.
12. To make the topping, in a mixing bowl, beat the heavy cream, powdered sugar, and vanilla extract until stiff peaks form. Spread the whipped cream over the chilled pie.
13. Optionally, garnish the pie with toasted coconut flakes before serving.
14. Slice and serve this delicious Coconut Cream Pie chilled, and enjoy the creamy, coconutty goodness!

Coffee Cake

Ingredients:

For the cake:

- 2 cups all-purpose flour
- 1 cup granulated sugar
- 1/2 cup unsalted butter, softened
- 2 large eggs
- 1 cup sour cream
- 1 teaspoon vanilla extract
- 1 teaspoon baking powder
- 1/2 teaspoon baking soda
- 1/4 teaspoon salt

For the streusel topping:

- 1/2 cup all-purpose flour
- 1/2 cup packed brown sugar
- 1 teaspoon ground cinnamon
- 1/4 cup unsalted butter, melted

For the glaze (optional):

- 1/2 cup powdered sugar
- 1-2 tablespoons milk or cream
- 1/2 teaspoon vanilla extract

Instructions:

1. Preheat your oven to 350°F (175°C). Grease and flour a 9x9-inch square baking pan or a 9-inch round cake pan. Set aside.
2. In a large mixing bowl, cream together the softened unsalted butter and granulated sugar until light and fluffy.
3. Add the eggs one at a time, beating well after each addition. Stir in the sour cream and vanilla extract until smooth.

4. In a separate bowl, sift together the all-purpose flour, baking powder, baking soda, and salt.
5. Gradually add the dry ingredients to the wet ingredients, mixing until just combined. Do not overmix.
6. In a small bowl, prepare the streusel topping by combining the flour, brown sugar, and ground cinnamon. Stir in the melted unsalted butter until the mixture resembles coarse crumbs. Set aside.
7. Spread half of the cake batter into the prepared baking pan, smoothing the top with a spatula.
8. Sprinkle half of the streusel topping over the batter in the pan.
9. Carefully spread the remaining cake batter over the streusel layer, and then sprinkle the remaining streusel topping over the batter.
10. Bake in the preheated oven for 35-40 minutes, or until a toothpick inserted into the center of the cake comes out clean.
11. Remove the cake from the oven and let it cool in the pan on a wire rack for 10-15 minutes.
12. If desired, prepare the glaze by whisking together the powdered sugar, milk or cream, and vanilla extract until smooth. Drizzle the glaze over the cooled cake.
13. Slice and serve the Coffee Cake warm or at room temperature, and enjoy with a cup of coffee or tea!